My Life and Travels in Belize

Marlon August

Dedicated to my late mother, Claribell Burns

and to my children, Melissa, Jamie, Marlon Jr. and Alinie.

Foreword

Like many great books, this one had its genesis during a conversation at a bar. In this case it was not just any bar, it was the Coco Locos beach bar in San Pedro, Belize. When I moved to Belize in 2006 Marlon August was among the first people I met. He was one of the bartenders at Coco Locos and we spent many days and nights in conversation and laughter. Sometime after his umpteenth story that had me amazed and entertained I suggested that he write down his experiences and put them into a book. What you are now reading is a result.

When you ask frequent visitors to Belize or expatriates who have moved there what makes them love the country so much you will likely hear the answer, "It's the people." It sounds cliche but it is a nearly universal observation of those familiar with the country. Belizeans are happy to meet you, to learn about you and to welcome you into their family almost as if you were kin.

In this regard Marlon August is a credit to his country. In his many careers he has met thousands of people and made close friends from all over the world. To those people and many more these stories will serve as a welcome return to the warm and often wild experiences heard while bending an elbow at a welcoming beach bar in one of the most beautiful corners of the world.

Pete Sisco

My name is Marlon B. August. I was born on the twenty-ninth of February in 1968 to Claribell Burns and Zachary August.

I was the last of fourteen children: Owen, Peter, Ramiro, Elvira, Angel, Zack Jr., Marigold, Richard, Maud, Simon, Walter, Elroy, Gilroy, and finally me.

My Youth in Belize

I was born to a large family, and I started off on my own when I was thirteen. I left home at thirteen and I went to Punta Gorda in search of work. I actually ran away from home because my mom wouldn't let me go on my own and I realized that my dad wouldn't support me, and I didn't want to run back from one parent to the other.

I ran away and got a job at a little village town called Toledo District, which is the rice capital of Belize. At the time, one of my brothers was running that rice mill. I didn't want him to know I was there and that I ran away.

I befriended one of his friends that he had brought to

our house one summer who owned a little restaurant bar. I rented a little room in the guest house in the back from her with money that I had saved working while I was going to grade school.

She said she would put me up for a couple weeks but that if my brother came around drinking, she wouldn't be able to hide me anymore.

I said, "That's fine. By then he won't be mad at me or bother me too much."

In fact, my mom was worried sick about me and back in those days there were only community phones, so if you wanted to communicate you called the community phone from one village to the next, and then you had to wait for a messenger boy to go tell the person they had a call, then you had to call again within fifteen minutes or so to speak to them.

My brother ended up taking me to his house to live, and then he made that call to my mom and let her know I was there. He said, "If you want to work, you can stay with me. You don't need to be renting a room from Ms. Rose."

So he kept me there and I worked at the sawmill for six months before I had a couple weeks off to visit my mom. I had all the money I had worked for and that I had been saving, so I paid the bills when I came home.

My mom would say, "Take some money and go out and have fun with your friends." I had a hard time trying to spend five bucks, so I would buy a couple buckets of popcorn, peanuts and soda and I'd still come home with change out of the five I took, and that's me and my friends.

I kept working at the saw mill until I got tired and I said, "There must be something better to do."

I ran into another brother who moved down there prior to me. He was married and he lived with his in-laws there. There was a guy who had an orange orchard right around the corner who needed help gardening and cleaning and stuff, so my brother and I worked with him for about nine months.

After that I decided I'd move on to another something. I got a job on the SeaLine bus service that was going from Punta Gorda to Belize City. I'd leave at five o'clock in the morning and then get to Belize City in the late hours of the afternoon. We wouldn't be able to make a return trip so we'd have to spend a night in Belize City and then go back the following day, and then we'd do it over again. It was like that every day. I'd meet my buddy on the road. It was a dirt road back in those days, before they got the asphalt.

I went to this place to work called VOA, Voice of America, a relay station they have down there at the end of Punta Gorda. It's a little area called Orange Point, but at the time it was just dirt and stuff so we did some land clearing. I worked for a guy who was an ex-representative, like a governor or something. We worked there for three or four months before we took a few days off, or a week off, and we had a guy from Belize City who was the foreman of the company.

So he'd go visit his family in Belize City and I'd hitch a ride with him, and we'd stop at the crossroads where he goes east and I go west. Then at the end of the week we would decide where we should meet. There were no cellphones in those days, so if I wasn't there when the ride was going through, I'd have to find my own way back, which was tough to do.

One time I was hiking because I had just gotten off and I'd missed my ride. I saw a Canadian guy who I ran into there, and a Venezuelan, and they'd been hiking three or four hours on the northern highway trying to get to the southern highway to get to a place halfway to Punta Gorda.

All of a sudden I saw this vehicle coming over the hill with a Belizean flag flying on it and I told the guy, "Don't worry. We've got a ride."

He said, "What do you mean, man? That looks like an official vehicle."

I said, "You bet it is. That's the prime minister of the country."

He said, "All right, then you're telling us that we're going to get a ride with the prime minister of the country? You've got to be shitting me."

I said, "No kidding, man. I'm telling you the truth."

I went out, stuck my thumb out and they guy stopped. It was a beat up old land rover, because that's the way the prime minister of the country was back then. His nickname was The Father of the Nation. He was and still is a very nice guy, he's about ninety years old now. He stopped and picked us up and he looked at me and said, "You're an August."

I said "Yes, Sir."

He said, "I might not be able to tell you what your first name is, but I can tell you who your daddy is."

I said, "Yes, sir."

He said, "Your father's name is Zachary August."

I said, "Yes, sir. That's him."

We continued to talk, and he told me about the time they used to work together at a plantation. He was a foreman and my dad was a worker there. They knew each other from back then.

While we were talking, the guy from Canada said, "Sir, it's been an honor. It's such a pleasure to get a ride with the prime minister of the country. My folks back home won't believe I did this," and so he asked him for an autograph.

They started talking and the prime minister asked, "What part of Canada are you from, young man?"

He said, "Sir, I'm from a little town you might not know. It's called Flin Flon, Manitoba."

The prime minister said, "Of course. I've been there, my boy. I've been to Calgary, I've been to Montreal, I've been to Quebec, I've been to all these places." Then he started speaking French to this guy and they carried on a conversation, because the prime minister is a multilingual guy. He speaks Italian, French, German, all sorts of languages.

The Venezuelan guy was sitting there with his mouth open he said, "When is my turn? I want to talk to this guy." He said that to me in Spanish and the prime minister started speaking Spanish to him.

The guy said, "Yes, sir. It's like this guy says. My folks back home will not believe that I was hiking through Belize and hitched a ride with the prime minister. May I get an autograph from you, and a photograph, sir?"

So they did that stuff and we continued on the journey to where we were going. He passed the village where he was supposed to be going for a council meeting. He just waved them by. He said, "I'll be right back. Wait for me. I'm just going to take my friends to the crossroad." It was like six miles out of his way, but he did that for us.

We hiked from there to a little village where we stopped and had drinks and stuff. When we got to the bar, the guys I was with went right from there to get a ride to where they were going.

I was stuck because I wouldn't take a ride hop since by this time it was already dark. So I was sitting there on my bag, waiting for a bus or something when a little old lady came by and said, "Son, what are you doing out here? You're going to get eaten up by the sun flies."

I said, "Ma'am, I have nowhere to go."

She said, "Well, come on in and stay with us and then you can keep hiking in the morning."

I said, "Well thank you, ma'am."

She took me to her house and I hung out there a little bit. She was trying to cook me something but I said, "No ma'am, it's okay. You don't have to go out of your way."

We sat down and started talking. She asked me my name and I said, "My name is Marlon."

She said, "No, what's your surname, young man?"

I said, "August."

She said, "So you're an August boy, are you?"

I said "Yes, ma'am."

She said, "Well, we have another August sleeping right back there. Do you think you two are related?"

I said, "I wouldn't know, ma'am."

So she asked her granddaughter to take me over there. Sure enough, I got over there and he really looked like me.

We got talking and backtracking. It was my second cousin, my dad's first cousin. So we talked and he said, "Well, you could stay with us."

They had a nice big house and they fixed me some food.

I woke up in the morning, continued my hike, and said my goodbyes. They said "Now listen, cuz. You ran into us by mistake, so don't let this be your last visit. You come on back and visit us."

I caught my ride in the morning, went down to my job, and started working again. And a few months later I went back home for another visit to see my mom.

Meeting Mary Alice

When I was working at Voice of America, I had just come home from work one day, walking through the town, and I was covered in grease and mud.

There was a girl from my hometown walking by, so I said, "Hey Stephanie. How are you doing?"

She wouldn't give me the time of day. But another girl was walking across the street, going to the store to do some shopping, and she said to me, "Hey, that girl didn't seem very friendly, did she?"

I said, "No ma'am. But you know, it's the way it is. A girl like her, dressed up in her uniform, doesn't want to say hi to a guy covered up in grease and mud."

I was on my way to see my boss to get a little money for the week, but she stopped to talk to me and I introduced myself. I said, "Hey, my name's Marlon."

She said, "I'm Mary Alice. You look like you could use a drink, Marlon. Why don't you go to my house over there and make yourself a drink? I'll be right back."

I walked over to her house and stood on the porch until eventually she came back and said, "Hey Marlon, why didn't you go in and make yourself a drink like I told you to?"

I said, "Ma'am, I wasn't raised that way. I don't enter somebody's house if they aren't there to open the door for me."

She said, "Well, that's a good quality, young man. But you can come in now."

I said, "Well, even so, I don't want to come into your house. I'm covered in mud and grease. I don't want to dirty your house."

She said, "Nah, don't worry about it. I've got a housemaid. She'll do the cleaning up."

I sat down and she made me a drink. We sat there for a while and had a few drinks together. She told me what her plans were, and that she needed some help.

I said, "Well, I'm here."

She said, "You've got a job. Whenever you're out of the job you've got now, you come see me."

I knew this could be a nice opportunity for me to be on top, the first boss or the foreman, so I decided to go back to work and get myself fired, even though I was working for one of my cousins and he was the boss. I'd go back to work where I was supposed to be digging holes, or mixing cement, or whatever, and I'd go lay around.

One day my boss came up to me and said, "Marlon, what's wrong with you? You look like you're not doing too good, like you're not willing to work. Why don't you go back home and when you're willing to work you can come see me."

I said, "Well, thank you sir. Can I get my check?"

He said, "Yeah, come into my office. I'll give you your money."

When I left I walked down to Mary Alice and said, "Hey Mary Alice, are you ready for me? Because I just got fired."

She said, "Oh, cool. I just got the lease going and stuff, and I'm ready to move out."

She had a pickup truck and a little sports car. She said, "You take the pickup truck and load shit in there, then take it to the house up there on the highway."

This was out in the country, and she was living in town. She said, "When we're done moving the stuff for the day, I'd like for you to spend the night there. I don't want anybody to go there and rip off the stuff we're taking there, and at the same time, I don't want to leave the other stuff here in town. So I'll spend the night down here at the house, and you go spend the night up there."

I took her up on the offer and I was sad that I did. The only good thing was that she had her own bar in the place where I was staying. But the place was haunted. I got there and there were all kinds of noises and stuff. I couldn't sleep. I lay down on the bed and it was all shaky, so I got up. We had no electricity. It was all hurricane lanterns.

I went into the kitchen and picked up a bottle of rum and just drank the whole thing, and by drinking all the rum I couldn't even tell whether there was anything supernatural going on because I was so passed out. The bed could shake all it wanted for all I cared.

The following day I went back to town and told her about it. She said, "You've got to be kidding me. There's no such thing as ghosts. There's no haunted house in Belize."

I said, "All right. Why don't we trade places? You go spend the night up there and I'll spend the night here in town."

She said, "All right, you're on."

Sure enough, she had the same experience.

So the third night we both spent the night there. We had moved everything by then. It was a four bedroom house, so I had two rooms to myself and she had two rooms to herself. Whatever went on, we would just say, "We don't mind." We sat around playing card games, drinking and smoking cigarettes, just relaxing and talking.

Then I made an explanation to her. I said, "You know what, Mary Alice? This place has been abandoned for a long time. It's a house from 1909 or something, and all the old folks who have lived and died here were buried in the yard."

The graveyard was covered in bushes, so I said, "Why don't we clean the graveyard and put out some flowers and stuff. That should keep the souls at peace."

So that's what we did, and sure enough, it kind of calmed everything down. It was our little haunted house and all the ghosts were friendly after that.

My Friend the Criminal

When I was working at Captain Morgan's, this guy named Gary used to come down and hang out in town. I lived in town at the time, so I used to go out and hang out at this little bar. And one day I went there and Gary was sitting there talking to the owner. They were negotiating some stuff, and Gary wanted to get a work permit in order to open a restaurant.

While they were talking, Gary wouldn't have anything to do with whatever the owner was offering, and that's because he wanted to become a citizen and everything and he wanted to do it cheap. So the owner told him, "Man, if you want to get all this done here within a year, give me thirty thousand dollars and I'll get it all done for you."

Gary said, "Come on, man. I'm not a rich guy. I want to do stuff legally and all that, so that I can get things going. I don't have that kind of money."

The owner said, "Oh man, you freaking cheap bastard," and walked away from him.

At the time, I had some good connections because my compadre was a consultant guy and he had his own farm for doing stuff like that, getting work permits for investor's and stuff, and he lived in Belize city.

So I said, "Hey Gary, come over here, man. Let me talk. I think I can help you."

He said, "Really?"

I said, "Yeah. There's this guy named Mark in Belize City who has an office that does stuff like this for investors. It will only take you a month or so to get everything set up, and it's going to cost you a little bit of money, but you could get it done."

He said, "How soon, man?"

I said, "As soon as you want. I mean, I can take you over there to meet him and he can do his stuff, and he'll tell you what you need to do to get set up."

He said, "All right."

So I asked for a day off at Captain Morgan's and went over to Belize city with him to meet my compadre and do the paperwork. We did that and my compadre took his passport and told him, "You need to go photocopy this, and photocopy that" and whatnot.

Within two weeks, he sent the guy his work permit and everything and he was ready to go. He had everything set after a couple weeks, so we went to Belize City and shopped for pots and pans and groceries and silverware and everything he needed to open this restaurant. Well, it seemed like that was the only money he had. He had no money to rent a place for the restaurant and he was renting a little apartment where the locals live for cheap.

All the time we'd come around his house and he'd invite us over for food and he'd make some egg salad and different sandwiches or something. It was a little weird because at the time I had only one daughter, she was like four or five, and we'd go over. Of course you can't leave a little girl at home by herself, so the wife and daughter came over with me when he said to come by, and I knocked at the door and he answered it stark naked.

I said, "Hey, what the hell's wrong with you? You called us over to come by. Why the hell don't you have clothes on? Put some clothes on, man. I got my little girl with me and everything."

He said, "All right, all right. It's so hot in here. I like to stay cool."

We went downstairs and waited for a while and when we came back up he had the table set. He was just all over the place with different ideas about inventions and stuff for divers. Contraptions for divers to take their wallets and sunglasses with them on a dive without getting them wet.

I said, "Gary, all right. You need to focus on the stuff you want to do with this restaurant. You can't be thinking about all this stuff at the same time. Wait till you get something going first, then get into something else."

He said, "Yeah, yeah, yeah. I guess that's a good idea."

We'd go and hang out at Captain Morgan's, or we'd go down to Capricorn when I was done with work and have a drink or two here and there.

One time we were hanging out at Capricorn sitting there having a drink and I made a mistake. I said to the guys, "This is one of my gringo buddies here."

He completely went off on me. He said, "Come on, Marlon! I'm no goddamn gringo! I'm Italian-Canadian! I'm not a gringo!"

I said, "Gary, it doesn't mean nothing derogative. Gringo is a term for any caucasian man, you know?"

He said, "Well, no. I don't think I'm classified as gringo because I'm Italian-Canadian, and that's a bad term."

I said, "All right, dude. I'm sorry. I won't call you that again."

He said, "Yeah, all right."

We sat and ate and drank and after that I thought, "Man, this guy has got a chip on his shoulder or something." But he seemed all right, so I didn't give up on him. Everybody knew me, and they knew I was hanging out with him.

We left and he went back to his apartment and I went home. I talked to my wife about what happened and she said, "You just have to keep a close eye."

After that event, I had his cell number he had mine, but we didn't contact each other for a while. I tried to contact him for two weeks and couldn't get a hold of him. His phone was turned off or something. He never tried contacting me and I'd go by his house now and then but he was never there. Another week went by and finally I get a call from him.

He said, "Hey, Marlon! You ready for some money?"

I said, "Well, it's about damn time. I invested some. I mean, I took a day off went to Belize City with you to get your work permit and everything. Where are you at?"

He said, "I don't know."

I said, "Gary what the hell do you mean, man? Where are you at?"

And he said, "I don't know!" And he hung up on me.

But he had asked me if I wanted some money so it certainly sounded like a promise that he was getting me some money. I didn't know what was his intention was, what he was doing, or what he was up to.

A day or two later, one of the managers from Captain Morgan's was in town to make a transaction at the bank. I got up on the boat and I heard people talking about something that had happened the day before.

I got to work and one of my managers said, "Man, did you hear about what happened? My mom and dad were witnesses. This guy tried to rob that bank."

At the time, the police station was adjacent to the Atlantic bank. I said, "You're kidding, man."

He said, "Nope."

And somebody else said, "Hey Marlon. The guy who robbed the bank is your buddy, man. The guy you used to hang out with, you know? He walked over in a leather jacket and black jeans and cowboy boots and tried to rob it."

I'd always figured he was a little weird, but I never expected anything like this. I said, "Goddamn. I hope he didn't spill my name when they arrested his ass and say he was hanging out with me, because I had nothing to do with it."

Fortunately, he didn't. But one of the bank managers was all shook up. He said, "This guy came in here, and after a few minutes there's people coming in from all corners. The whole town was scattered around here." This was after Gary had been arrested and buckled up.

What happened was when he entered the bank, he asked to see the manager. They sent him upstairs, and under his jacket all he had was a Maglite. He walks up to the manager upstairs and said, "I'd like to have eighty thousand dollars in US currency, unmarked bills," and some money in Belizean, I think.

The manager played it cool fiddled around under his desk like he was getting something. This guy was so dumb, because downstairs was a camera and TV monitor and a guy down there could see what was going on. The security downstairs have a secret code or alarm. So the guy hit the alarm button downstairs and the security guard, who was armed, ran upstairs right away and stuck the guy up. The other guard went over to the police station and grabbed the cops, and they came over.

They marched him downstairs outside of the bank, right onto the main street, and all the cops came over and grabbed him and his blue Maglite. They found out that was all he had under his jacket. So that was the news on the island for about a week, and everybody was saying to me, "You knew this freaking guy who tried to rob the Atlantic bank!"

He hadn't had an escape plan or anything. He was just going to rob the bank and walk down the street. That's what he thought. Everyone was saying, "He's so stupid. Right next to the police station. He doesn't even have a car out there. He has nothing."

As a matter of fact, they all said he would have needed a helicopter to get off the island if he wanted to rob the bank like that.

That was part of what happened when they questioned him in court and they asked him, "What was your plan?"

He said, "I don't know. I just needed some money, so I

figured I'd go rob a bank. I didn't know it was *that* dumb, you know? I didn't have any backup plans."

They took his ass to Hattieville and they left him up there for about eight months before his case was tried. The judge checked him out and they had psychiatrists examine him and, sure enough, they pleaded insanity and they agreed to that.

They sent him to psychiatric treatment and then they moved him to board him back to Canada. That was the last I've heard or seen of Gary.

Bar Fight with a Machete

On one occasion I was coming back home from work in Merida. I had a friend who came and spent a couple weeks with me buying jewelry because he was a jeweler. He said it was cheaper in Merida, and he turned it into good profit when he brought it back to Belize.

So he was there with me for about fifteen days and we were both coming back to Belize, and we were glad to be coming back. As soon as we got off the bus he said, "Marlon, man. I'm ready for a good Belizean beer. Belikin, man. I'm sick and tired of those damn Mexican beers."

So we stopped in a very bad neighborhood bar and I

said, "Clarence, we can't stop and have a beer here, man. This is a bad bar man. I know this place in downtown Belize City."

But he said, "No, man. I know the owner. I have a couple of rings for him that he ordered from me, so let's go in here."

Sure enough we went in, and we were having fun and drinking beers, and I wouldn't leave now because they had my WWE on the TV—although this was back then it was called WWF. It's wrestling stuff, and I'm a big fan of that. So I was staying there and watching that until it was finished, and he and I were having fun.

Then, about halfway through this, there was a guy sitting there with a girl. He seemed to be having a problem with her, and she seemed to be having a problem with him. They were just sitting there and she looked like she needed somebody to talk to, or somebody who could afford to buy her a drink.

After a little while the guy went to the bathroom, and some friends of mine from LA, Belizean-Americans, came in and said, "Hey, Marlon. We haven't seen you for a while. What are you doing here?"

I said, "I just came in from Merida, having a drink."

They said, "So let's buy you one."

I said, "Well I've got a full one right now, but if you want to put one in the well for me I'll gladly appreciate it."

They did and then they asked me, "What's up with the girl?"

I said, "Man, I mean, she seems to be lonely. This guy's sitting there, not buying her a drink. Go talk to her. Maybe you're the kind of guy she would prefer to hang out with."

My friends did, and one of them said something to the girl and sure enough, they picked up and left.

But while they were gone, after a while, the guy came back from the restroom. He looked around, doesn't see his girlfriend, came straight to me and said, "Man, where'd my girlfriend go?" He didn't speak English well or anything.

I said, "Man, don't be messing with me. I'm not here to secure nobody for nobody, you know. Find her on your own, or talk to the bartender."

So I was just sitting there watching wrestling and he got mad and pushed me and said, "You know something you don't tell me."

I told him, "Man, just leave me alone."

The bartender saw that he was bugging me, and he knew the guy's character, so he came and shoved him out of the bar and closed the gate. The guy got madder and started yelling and screaming at me in Spanish, saying that he was going to come back for me and that he's going to go get his machete, stuff like that.

I paid no mind. I just kept watching my wrestling and figured he was bluffing anyway.

Well a guy went out and locked this gate, or at least I thought he had put the lock on, but he didn't. So in a few minutes, the guy came back, rattling the chain that was wrapped around the gate and he got it lose. And now he had the machete.

I didn't pay much attention. I thought he couldn't get through, and I was deep in my wrestling when I realized what was happening.

My friend nudged me and said, "Look Marlon!"

He was aiming to chop me in the head over this little stuff. I put my hand up and he cut my thumb open. I jumped up and, defending myself in reflex, I cracked my Belikin bottle on the bar and jammed him in the ribcage. I knocked him off his feet and he hit his head on the concrete floor.

But now my thumb was cut open, almost off, and I was just pissed. I mean, I was furious. I jumped on his chest and start pounding him, and I pounded him in the face until his face swelled up like a football, and I kicked him in the ribs again and again. I had white pump Reeboks on at the time and I kicked him so much my white Reeboks turned red.

After a little bit, the bartender came up and tried to stop the fight, grab the machete, pull me away from him and everything. He couldn't even get the machete anyway, because I had him on the ground. I was choking the shit out of him and the bartender said, "No, man. You're going to kill him!"

I said, "Yeah, that's what I want to do. I want to kill his ass. Son of a bitch."

Damn Honduran guy, you know. One of them had just killed one of my brothers a few years ago. I said, "One's trying to kill me now? No way. I want to make an example of this son of a gun here."

Somebody managed to get me off him, and people around the bar, a couple guys I knew from back home, were saying, "Man, Marlon you better get out of here because the cops are going to be here and stuff, and they're going to drag you in and pin you down for the night.".

So I say, "All right."

I grabbed a taxi cab guy and he took me to his house to clean up my wounds and stuff. He said, "Don't go seeking medical attention until the morning, because if you go tonight they'll definitely know it was you that was in the confrontation with that guy."

So I didn't go until morning, but I went. Sure enough, even though I went the following day, they questioned me.

"Were you in a fight at the such and such bar? You know a guy came in here with broken ribs, and lacerations and stuff, a swollen face, and broken jaw and all that?"

I said, "No, doctor. I was sharpening my machete and I slipped and cut myself."

He said, "All right."

I said, "As a matter of fact, I'm paying social security. You guys are supposed to take care of me, not interrogate me. You guys aren't the cops."

They said, "No, no, man. We were just wondering, you

know."

And I said, "All right."

They took care of me, stitched me up and everything, and I went on back to my work.

How My Brother Lost His Eye

When Gilroy lost his eye, he was about ten or eleven years old. He was one of the twins, and my mom was sewing at the time. We had friends down the road about three miles from where we grew up and my mom was sending the other twin, Elroy, there to gather some coconuts. Elroy was on his way already, and Gilroy started crying, "Mom, can I go with him? Mom, can I go with him?"

I told her, "Mom, you shouldn't let him go, because something bad is going to happen," but she just didn't want him to be bugging her while she was doing her sewing, so she said "All right, go. But if anything happens to you, don't blame me."

Sure enough, we went there to help our brother gather coconuts. He was peddling around the farmyard and stuff.

This guy had just come in for lunch with his tractor, and he left it running to go grab a quick lunch before going back and plowing the fields. So he had the tractor with the plow attached and the engine was on. So my brother went and started fiddling with the levers, and he yanked on some lever that catapulted him head first onto the plow and cut his head open like a can.

At the time, the highway was still a little rocky dirt road, so the bus would take a very long time to go three miles, especially when it was full and had a lot of pit stops to make.

They saw him covered in blood. My other brother had found him, grabbed him and they got on the bus coming home. When they got there, my mom was sitting on the veranda and saw that my brother was covered in blood. She just jumped over the veranda railing, which was about fifteen feet from the ground, and ran and grabbed my brother and hugged him. The next truck going up to town, she hitched a ride and took him to the hospital.

Fortunately one of my brothers was working right across from the hospital, and if it wasn't for him my brother would have died that day. The doctor said because he had bled out so much he needed blood right away to save his life. So they yanked blood out of my older brother and put it right in, without screening or anything, and he went on like that and got well. The wound healed. For weeks and months, we kept going back to the doctor and they'd have to check him up and stuff.

He would keep complaining to my mom about migraine headaches, and back then we only had candlelight and lanterns, which he liked to read by. So my mom would say, "Well, it's because you're reading by candlelight that you're getting all those headaches."

So she'd take him back to the doctor and the doctor would check on his migraine, but he didn't do anything about it for about two weeks. Later on, he realized that my brother was suffering from eye problems, because he had a cut. So he said to my Mom, "Well, you'll have to take this boy to see an eye specialist."

But it was a little too late for that, because two weeks later, the nerve from the eye had already died. So my mom took him to the eye specialist and this is exactly what the eye specialist said: "I'm sorry, ma'am. If you had brought him a couple weeks earlier, we could have saved his eye, but it's just too far gone now."

So that's how my brother lost his eye.

Fun with Gurkhas

I used to come home from working on my holidays from Punta Gorda. I would stay around my hometown, and there would be a lot of parties going on.

Melchor is a little border town in Guatemala across from Belize. It was illegal for any British soldiers in Belize to cross over because it was enemy territory. Well, they had the Gurkhas, who were soldiers from Nepal that were in the British army. They were basically snipers who would cut peoples' necks open with a knife. They're mean little bastards. They're small people but mean little bastards.

One day I smuggled about five of them across the water

to have fun with girls and stuff like that. We were out there having fun and stuff, and all of a sudden I saw a bunch of Guatemalan soldiers coming up towards the bar where I was hanging out with these Gurkhas. So I said, "Guys, it's time to go. Let's roll."

This was around two o'clock in the morning and we headed through the jungle and stuff. I always had a guy there close to the river who had a canoe and could take us across the river. When it wasn't too flooded or too high, we could kind of swim across it. At this point in time it was too flooded, so I went and got this guy and jumped in the canoe.

As soon as we got across, we saw the Guatemalan soldiers come through with their lights. We headed up toward the hill on the Belize side and looked through the bushes and there they were.

The Gurkhas would have gotten shot or arrested, and I probably would have too, but we escaped that one.

We came right back through the river to Guatemala and kept partying. These guys probably partied until four or five in the morning. They rode on the ferris wheel and stuff like that. These guys had a blast.

They said, "Thank you, Marlon. We didn't believe we would be able to go to enemy territory and have fun."

We enjoyed ourselves there on the other side, then came back down to Belize and they said their goodbyes. They all gave me a little something.

The Overdose

While I was working at Capricorn one time, this lady came in. She had rented a sailboat after meeting a guy in Miami. They had just come down on vacation together. She was really shifty from the time she came in, having two sets of traveler's checks and different names on her passports, you know, she had two passports.

Well, they sat around for a while. She had a lot of money. She invited all her crew members to dinner, rented a sailboat, and they were just sitting around having fun.

I was bartending, and she came up and said, "You have Stout?"

I said, "Yes ma'am, I do."

She said, "Well I'd like a Stout, and give everybody else what they want."

Her boyfriend came and had a rum punch, and the guys all had beers. We were busy at Capricorn. It was one of the top places to dine at the time and all the tables were full and people were dining, eating and drinking wine.

She took one sip of her Stout and said, "I need the restroom."

We only had two restrooms at the time, one for ladies and one for men, and this lady after having one sip of Stout went to the bathroom and she locked herself in for about half an hour.

My boss thought maybe somebody had locked the door before they pulled it closed. Since he didn't have any keys to open it from the outside, he had to go get a screwdriver to unlock the door, and while he was doing that we heard: "Hey! Can't a woman have a minute in here?"

I said, "Ma'am you've been in there half an hour. There are other people that need to use the restroom."

So she came out and came back to the bar, looked at me and said, "Where's my drink?"

I said, "It's sitting right there."

She said, "I'm not going to drink that. Give me another one."

I said, "Okay ma'am, but I'm telling you, you drank that and left it there. I'm going to have to charge you."

She said, "I don't care. Give me another one!"

I gave her another one and she went and sat with her crowd. In a little while, halfway through her second drink, she walked up to the bar again and said, "Where's the restroom?"

I said, "Ma'am, it's right in there. You were just there a little while ago."

She said, "Don't be smarting off with me!"

I said, "Okay, I'm sorry."

She went into the bathroom again and locked herself in for another half an hour. So Clarence had to bust the door open with a screwdriver. When he did that, he found the lady in there and again she said, "Can't a lady have a minute in the restroom here?"

"Ma'am, you've been in here for half an hour," is what Clarence said to her. Then she came out, and she walked straight to the bar all dazed, with her eyes all rolled up in her head, and she started turning green. The boyfriend, who was sitting there waiting for her, held her and walked her out on the beach. But she left her Stout sitting at the bar.

We had a full restaurant full of people. The deck was all full of people dining. There was this guy, Dr. Paul, a doctor from somewhere in the States, having dinner there. And as soon as this guy took this lady out on the beach, they hugged each other, and the lady started shaking up, having a seizure. They were hugging, so everybody thought they were just doing it there on the beach. But eventually she fell to her knees, dropped down, and everyone saw her showing a seizure. Dr. Paul jumped over the balcony to rescue her and this dive master, Steve Bowen, went out there and tried to render assistance by doing CPR and all this other stuff.

The doctor looked at the lady and he saw that she was turning green and said, "You don't need to. This lady is breathing. You don't need to do CPR. All you need to do is get a spoon and put it in her mouth so she doesn't bite her tongue or something."

A little while after that, Annabelle and Clarence came out and realized this lady was dying on their property. So they put her on a stretcher—they used the board I used to close the bar as a stretcher. At this point in time Annabelle wasn't used to driving a boat at night, so she grabbed a staff guy who cleaned the yard and stuff, and said, "You stay onboard the boat, at the front, with a light, you know, and hold it."

It was maybe a month or so that they had been trying to set up the area for a dock for deep water so a boat could come in and dock. There was a little sand bottom out there a ways, that wasn't usually there. Well, with all the speed and stuff trying to get the lady to the medical facilities, Annabelle hit the ground there and flung the guy off the boat. It was a good thing he was holding onto the rope. He just went underneath the boat, and they dragged him for a bit until the boat slowed down and he let go, but he didn't get chopped up by the prop.

So he swam ashore and it was pitch black and his flashlight was gone, so nobody could find him. After they circled a few times he started yelling out that he was okay and they picked him up and took the lady and continued the journey toward town.

If she wasn't dead of the overdose by now, she was already dead from all that time waiting to get to the doctor.

Finally they got to the doctor's office—it was called

"Lion's Clinic" at the time—and they walked the lady in, the boyfriend carrying her on his shoulder, and while they were walking they called the doctor and walked in through the door, and the boyfriend spun around and whacked the lady's head on the edge of the door. So if she wasn't dead already, she was definitely dead now.

As soon as the doctor had a look at her and studied all of her skin and her face, he said "Let me see her purse." When he opened the purse there was all kinds of blood-soaked tissues and needles and stuff to give away that she was on drugs and that she was shooting up with something.

So he said, "You know what? This lady has OD'd. She's dead. Why did you bring her here? Just take her away from here. I have no place to put her." So they went and called the place they were staying, a Bed and Breakfast, and they asked for a favor. So the lady there cleaned out the stand in fridge and put the dead lady in there.

So other ladies came in in the morning to prepare

breakfast and they weren't aware of what's going on. They were used to having vegetables and fruits and stuff in the fridge. So one of them opened up the stand in cooler and an arm fell out. She started running, and she ran and got to the police station saying, "There's a dead lady in the fridge!"

A little happened after that. They had to have an investigation and stuff, and they said, "You can't be running a Bed and Breakfast with a dead body in the cooler," so they had to close the place down for a little bit, and after that and clean the place up.

There was a stink all over the island, though. Everyone knew about it. They couldn't have business anymore for a long, long time.

Acting in a Movie

There was a movie being filmed at Ramon's. It was called "Object of Desire" with Traci Lords. At the time, I was a bartender and a security guard at night, so I had about three hours to relax during the day.

Coming home from my security shift one morning, this lady walked up to me and said, "Hey guy, how would you like to be in a movie?"

I said, "Listen, ma'am. Don't be telling me no dreams. People come over here all the time trying to invite me to the States. They don't give me a ticket, they don't send me anything, they just say 'Come on. I've got an apartment, and I've got a car waiting for you.'"

She said, "No, no, no, guy. I'm not one of those people. As a matter of fact, it's being filmed right here. I'm not trying to take you to the States. If you don't believe me, go and check it out at Ramon's."

I said, "All right."

So I went to check it out and sure enough she wasn't bullshitting me. It was good. I went up to the director and I said, "Hey, how are you? I'm Marlon. I met this girl and she said to check over here about a spot in this movie you guys are doing."

Back then I had a six-pack and long hair. I looked like a rebel. They wanted me for this part where I had to sit at a bar and punch this guy off a barstool.

They hired me, so for my three hours of break during the day I was there doing my scene. I'd wait for my part to come, then I'd punch this guy off the bar stool. After that, they had me walk on the beach with a couple of bikini girls and play volleyball in the background.

That wasted about three or four months. Eventually they caught the director with cocaine, and they fired the whole crew for doing illegal stuff. After that, as far as I know, they went to finish the movie in Mexico.

In San Pedro, 2012

Sailing with family and friends

As a tour guide at the Belize Zoo

Taking a break on the seawall

Adventures in America

This girl I knew by the name of Mary Alice had plans to go back to Florida because she had run out of money, and she took me with her. She owed me a year's salary that I had worked for. She said she was keeping it in the well, but the well went dry from her throwing parties every other weekend.

She would throw parties and invite the merchants from town, trying to be accepted into the community. That didn't work in her favor because nobody would chip in. She just spent her money, including mine, and the well went dry, so to speak.

In the midst of that, she said, "Marlon, I'm going to have to go back to Florida and get a job because I don't have any money for you, but in the meantime you can take that pickup truck as a down payment."

I said, "Mary Alice, I'm eighteen years old. There is no Belizean guy who would want to have a pickup truck at eighteen years old, let alone be able to afford the gas for it.

It was a damn good pickup truck—beefed up, big wheels and everything. It could pass everything on the road except the gas station with that V8 engine, but back then gas was expensive.

She said, "Well, what do you want me do?"

I said, "Just sell the truck and take me to the States with you. That would be payment enough."

So she did that, and we went to Florida where her parents and brothers and sisters and everybody got to know me. I was there having a good time, hanging out for three months, going to Disney World, SeaWorld, the Kennedy

Space Center, all the fun stuff in Florida.

After three months of that, I was bored sick. I said that I wanted to go back, but being that they were family they said, "No, Marlon. You can't leave just yet." Her dad was in immigrations, so he kept stamping my passport to get me more time in the States.

Eventually I said "If I'm going to stay here any longer, I want to have a job."

We were living in Tampa and she called up a friend at her flying service up in Ft. Lauderdale. The guy said, "Sure. I'll give it a run if he can do the job."

So I went up to Ft. Lauderdale on Monday mornings and stayed at a hotel there, and I would work at night. That way there were fewer immigrations guys coming from the airplane. In the midst of all that I was supposed to tell people I was from some other country, because I didn't want to get caught by immigration.

Of course, there were guys there working. There was

one guy who had family in the country I was pretending to be from, but when he heard me talking he said, "That's not your real accent. Where the hell are you from?"

I said, "It's not any of your concern, but if you want to blow the whistle on me, I am from Belize. I am from Central America."

He says, "Yeah man, I have friend who could use this job, but you're working here illegally instead."

I said, "Listen. It's not up to me and you. It's up to your boss. If you have a problem, then you go talk to your boss. He's the one who hired me."

He went off on me and wanted to kick my butt. He was a big guy, two hundred and seventy-five pounds, maybe six foot four. At the time I was a skinny guy, about a hundred and sixty-four pounds soaking wet.

I said, "You know what? I'm not scared of you. I'll have to prove to you how tough I am, because down in Belize we fight with machetes and stuff like that. We work in the fields. Our lawnmowers are machetes. So it doesn't matter to me how big you are and how much pain you can inflict, because I know I can handle it. But when I turn back, you won't be able to handle it."

He said, "Yeah, well step it up. Bring it on."

I grabbed a knife and cut my own hand. It freaked him out. He dropped to his knees and said, "Man, don't be doing that to yourself. Goddamn! I didn't mean to push you over the edge. I really didn't. Just leave me alone."

I hurt myself so badly I was off the job for a month. My hand got so swollen I called my mom in Belize to ask her what to do, since I didn't have social security or anything and I couldn't go to a doctor.

I sat at home in Florida doing the hot and cold water and stuff like that. While I was homesick, Mike, the guy I'd had the confrontation with drove his Ninja bike down from Ft. Lauderdale to visit me and apologize for pushing me over the edge.

He said, "Marlon, man. I am so sorry. Let me take you out to dinner just to show you how bad I feel, how sorry I am about what I did."

I said, "All right."

I got dressed up in long sleeves and cufflinks and everything so he could take me to a fancy restaurant where they had a dress code. I'm a little Caribbean boy where there's no such thing as a dress code, so it was a little new to me. We went into the restaurant and got the menus and a couple drinks and he said, "Don't you worry about it. Anything you want. Money isn't an object. Anything you want. I'm so sorry."

I said, "All right, good, Mike. There is lobster here. Can I order that?"

He said, "Like I said, anything you want."

I ordered myself a lobster and they set it down at the table and brought all these instruments and utensils, crackers, knives, forks, this and that.

I said, "Listen, buddy. Is this food paid for?"

He said, "Yes, it is."

I said, "Do you mind if I devour it the way I know how?"

He said, "No worries, man."

So I grab the lobster and twist it and crack it and stuff, without using the proper utensils. The whole restaurant went into an uproar, and I said, "Don't mind me, I'm from Central America. I'm like Crocodile Dundee. This is my first trip to the United States. This is the way we eat. I'm going to eat my food, but I don't want to be fancy about it."

So we ate and had fun and he drove me back home. He said, "Marlon, I got friends here in Tampa that I am going to spend the night with. You get well soon. Sorry to push you over the edge. Let's be friends from now on."

I just said, "Sure Mike, no problem."

After that whole ordeal, I went back to work and my boss, whose name was also Mike, said, "Marlon, seeing as you're bilingual and you speak proper Spanish, I've got a deal going on in Venezuela and I need you to fly out there with me to talk to these guys so you can translate what I say to them."

It was a drug deal, so I said, "Boss, I appreciate you having me working here illegally, and I appreciate the offer but I have to say no to that. I don't want to screw up and have to be looking over my shoulder all the time."

He says, "Okay, you said no to me. But don't utter a word about this deal to anybody, not even your good friend Mary Alice who brought you here."

I said, "No sir. I appreciate the money you're paying me to work here and I wouldn't ever ever have anything to say about it. My lips are sealed when it comes to that."

He said, "Okay."

Within a couple weeks he did the deal with some little Cuban guy he found down in Miami. Everything worked out fine. When he came back he said to me, "That little

Cuban guy made about a quarter of a million US dollars that you were supposed to make."

I said, "Well that's good for him, sir. Maybe he has some starving family back in Cuba he can help now. I appreciate that you have me working and that I am making my money. Maybe he has done that before and knows exactly what to do."

I kept doing my regular routine work at this place and after about nine months I got homesick and told Mary Alice, "I'm done with this place. I want to go back home."

She said, "No. You should stay and become a US citizen!"

I said, "No, Mary Alice. I'm already an American citizen. I'm Central American, for God's sake."

She said, "Okay."

She was holding onto my passport because she had told immigrations and the people in Belize that she had just started a business and she needed some farm equipment to be brought into the country. She said she was bringing me up to get her the farm equipment and bring it back down.

They had made that deal and she had taken me under her wing, like she was my guardian, since in the US you have to be twenty one to legally be an adult.

She didn't want to bring me back to Belize so I told her if she didn't, I'd report her to the cops. Then she would be in trouble with the government, police, and United States.

So she brought me back, and as soon as we got to the airport in Belize City she said, "Marlon, let's bury the hatchet and just go back. You don't even need to go through customs. We can get back on the plane and go home."

I said, "Mary Alice, you're crazy. I'm home where I'm free and can do whatever I want. I don't have to worry about getting caught up in the rat race in the US with the rules and regulations they have there."

She said, "Well, if that is what you want, if your mind is made up, then so be it."

We went through customs and immigrations, and because I'm Belizean I got through faster than she did. She had already made arrangements for a cab to pick us up because she had no papers here, but I met a friend of my oldest brother that was there.

He said, "Hey, aren't you Peter August's brother?"

I said, "Yes, that is my older brother."

He said, "Where are you heading to?"

I said, "Well, I just want to get away from the airport and down to Belize city. Would you mind giving me a ride?"

He said, "Sure."

I threw my suitcase in the car and Mary Alice came running out and screaming, "Marlon, what are you doing? We have a cab waiting for us."

I said, "Well, you take the cab. I'm going with my brother's friends here."

He says, "That's the lady you came here with?"

I said, "Yeah, but I don't want anything to do with her."

He said, "Come on, man. We're Belizean. We're cool people. Let her take a ride with us."

I said, "Okay, if she wants to come with us, that's fine."

We drove back to town where my mom was hanging out with one of my older brothers in Belize City. My mom was shocked to see me coming out to the house because she didn't know I was coming back from the States.

She hugged me and Mary said, "Okay, I'll see you soon. I've got to go to immigrations to take my passport and stamp it in. I'll see you in a bit."

I told my mom everything that went on, and then Mary came to the house with my brother and he talked to her on the outside porch. She gave him her side of the story, and he believed her and came in after she left to try to lecture me.

I said, "Listen, man. You have no control over my life; I do what I have to do. She screwed me over, so I came back. She told you otherwise, and if you want to believe it, that's up to you. I am just happy to see my mom, and that I have enough money to go do whatever I want to do. I'm going to leave some money with my mom, and I am going to go travel a bit."

I had enough money to travel for six months, so I spent it traveling around Central America, then I came back to Belize and started working.

Confronting Diego

When I met Mary Alice she had come down because she'd had a run in with a drug lord from Corozal who was born in Belize. He had a bad run in with the cops in Florida and was shot up and hospitalized while Mary Alice was the head nurse taking care of him.

After years of their ordeal, she came to Belize because he had talked so much about the place. Knowing that he was from Corozal, she decided to go to Punta Gorda, which is southside on the opposite end of the country from Corozal. Little did she know that Diego had moved down the beach and opened a business there.

So while I was working at Voice of America and ran into her, she asked me if I wouldn't mind working for her. I went to work with her. During the time that I worked for her, she had me stay outside of town. She had a rented house in town. Days went by, weeks, months, whatever.

After a while, Diego found out that it was her and that a guy named Marlon was working for her. When she ran out of money and left the country, I went with her, and when I came back Diego thought I had snuck her out of the country and that I was protecting her from him. They had this old beef that he wanted to take care of. I had never even met the guy, but all of a sudden he wanted to kill me.

I went to hang out with friends, and his brother and I knew each other. All of my friends said, "You're a brave man to be hanging out here, Marlon. Diego has a headhunter on you and you're still hanging out here."

I said, "Well I didn't do anything to the guy. If he's got a headhunter on me he's barking up the wrong tree. He should be taking it out on Mary Alice. She did him wrong ten years ago."

I stayed in Punta Gorda for a little while. I didn't really come back to hang out there, I just came to visit friends when I got back from the States. So after that I went on a tour. I had made enough money in Florida, so after that I went to Guatemala, El Salvador, and other Central American countries. I did that for about six months.

After that I came back to hang out in my hometown, and there were always these football games—the rest of the world called them football—and there would always be a competition between my village and other villages. They had this big game that was between my village and the village that Diego is from, and it was going to be held in his village.

So I went there, and I had a cousin that lived up there in Corozal. I hooked up with my cousin and we went to the game together.

I said, "Hey, I know Diego is here for the game. I want you to point him out for me. I want to know who the hell this guy is. He's got a headhunter on me and I want to know him before he knows me."

He knew my name, but he didn't know what I looked like, so sure enough we were hanging back at the corner and Diego, his dad, and his brother walked right in front of my cousin and me.

My cousin said, "That's him," without letting them hear him.

After they'd walked by I said, "Which one, the one on the left, middle, or right?"

He said, "The one on the left with the curly hair and light skin."

I said, "All right, cool."

So now I knew who he was. I decided I was going to have to approach him one of these days in broad daylight and talk to him in public to let him know I didn't have anything to do with him and Mary Alice back in the day, and that he shouldn't be wanting to kill me or anything.

After the game, I went back down to Punta Gorda for the same reason: to meet him and let him know he shouldn't be trying to kill me, because I didn't do anything wrong. I went to his dad's grocery and hardware store, and I said to his brother behind the cash register, "Good morning, Fonso. Is your brother Diego at home?"

He said, "Yeah, he's upstairs. What do you want with him?"

I said to Fonso, "I want to make peace with Diego. I'm Marlon, the guy that he's looking for."

Fonso started laughing and said, "You've got balls, man. You don't know my brother."

I said, "Well that's why I came here. To make peace. I'm not scared. I just didn't do anything wrong, so he has no reason to want to hurt me."

He came downstairs, and I stuck my hand out and said,

"Good morning, Diego. My name's Marlon."

He said, "You're the Marlon who has been hanging out with Mary Alice?"

I said, "Yes, I am," but I didn't let go of his hand for one second. I said, "Listen, man. Me and you have no problems; I just wanted you to know. I came to you man to man just to let you know that I have nothing to do with whatever happened between you and Mary Alice ten years ago. I wasn't her friend then, I've just been her friend since she came here. If you have a past with her and you need revenge on her, go right ahead, be my guest, because I have nothing to do with her. I left her in the States, then I came back here, and she'll be back. She has plans to come back and rent a restaurant and bar and get something going, so you can get at her when she comes back."

He said, "Well thank you man, because if I didn't know, if you didn't come to me, I surely could have had you killed."

I said, "No worries, man. You don't have to worry about me."

And he said, "All right."

We made peace and parted ways.

Bar Fight Over the Movie Girls

Here is another story about when I was working on the set of the movie "Object of Desire" here in San Pedro. I had been walking home from work one day when I had run into this lady who said, "How would you like to be in a movie?" and I had said "Sure."

After working on the movie one night, I went partying at this event down at Tacklebox, which was a happening spot in town. I walked in there with two girls who I'd met on the movie set. They were both from the mainland and they were used to walking barefoot.

I went there, and I had my tennis shoes on, and I was

partying, dancing, and after a while one of the girls said, "Let's take a break, because the band took a break anyway. Let's go over to the bar and grab a drink."

I said, "Okay, go ahead. I'll meet you there in a minute. I want to sit down by these guys and take the sand out of my shoes."

So I bent over to take the sand out of my shoes and WHAM! Somebody whacked me in the ear. I shook it off, got the sand out of my shoes, put them back on, and made one big step forward, then I spun around and looked at the guys. I could tell one of them wasn't guilty of hitting me, so I accused him just to see what the other guy's reaction would be.

I argued with them a bit and eventually I said, "Man, just lay off me. I don't want you guys messing with me like that."

What had set these guys off was that they thought I should be sharing the girls with them, but the girls just wanted to hang out with me. They didn't want anything to do with these guys.

He approached me and stepped up like he wanted to throw a right hook at me, so as a reflex I uppercut him and sent him right through the glass window in the back. Back then they had a shark pit with all these sharks and things in there. It was a good thing he didn't fall into there or he would have been in real trouble.

Anyway, the girls and I walked out and security grabbed me. I said, "Man, you don't understand. A whole bunch of guys were messing with me."

So we walked out and I said, "Ladies, we might as well call it a night."

They said, "No, come on. We can't. Not because we had a little problem with this one place and those guys. We can keep partying. Let's go to the other place."

So we went to Big Daddy's, where we went dancing again and stuff. And sure enough, we were in there for half an hour when the same guys showed up. A few of them came inside, but I didn't know that there were others waiting outside.

The guy came up to me and I said, "Hey, you keep harassing me, man. I'm just trying to have fun and you come in here messing up my thing."

He said, "I want to finish this. Let's go outside."

I said, "All right."

We went outside and as soon as I got out, his buddy had a gun pointed at my head. So I was standing there shaking in my tennis shoes.

After a while, this guy came by who saw us and just by reflex, he knocked the gun out of the guy's hand. I grabbed him and put him in a chokehold, and as soon as I did that the guy's older brother came by and kicked me in the ribs. So I let go of the guy I had by the neck and chased after the brother.

He ran out toward the beach to the end of a dock. I ran

after him and he ran like a coward right into the water. I stood there waiting and said, "You come back out, you son of a bitch!"

He wouldn't come back. He swam a ways over to the next dock and got out from there.

The Barracuda

Back in 1989 or 1990 or so, I went spear fishing with one of the guys I worked with one day. I grew up in the rain forest, so I had no knowledge of how to go around in the ocean and catch fish. I had the lore that I'd gained listening to the old guys sit around and talk about their old experiences.

There was a guy who worked with us, his name was Bill. He was a great musician, a saxophone player, the best in the country of Belize at the time. He'd blow that saxophone until he had a hernia. He loved it. He used to entertain us. He was always out on the sea, too.

He told us one time a story about barracudas. If you're ever spear fishing and you catch one of them in the head, it's like hitting an anvil, and it will always get them mad and make them come back after you. You had to hit them directly in the stomach.

Well, we went spear fishing. The guy I was with hit one in the head, the same way that Bill had warned us about. His rod fell down to the sand floor, so he asked me to get him his spare. I motioned to him that I wasn't going to do that, and that I was instead going back up to the boat. I was the bagman. I had to take the fish and put them in the bag.

No sooner had I got up to the boat than my friend had gone to get his rod back. I saw blood all over the water. The barracuda had come around and chomped the guy on the foot, taking two of his toes off. I had to bring him back into the boat and get him back to the island.

It was a good thing we had a private plane with a pilot always on the premises. He flew him back to Belize City and got him fixed up and stuff, since he'd lost a lot of blood and gotten injured pretty badly.

To this day, that guy is still walking around Belize City. Every now and then when I go to Belize City I'll see him.

So on that note: Be careful if you're ever out there swimming in the ocean. Don't trust those barracudas.

\

The Sanchez Family

Prior to me working at the VOA where I met Mary Alice, I met this guy named Glen Sanchez. I was working at a little meat shop and grocery, and at that time we used to make a lot of trips from Belize City to Punta Gorda to bring in groceries.

Glen and I were working for this guy named Wallace. I was living fourteen miles out of town, where I worked. I used to hitch a ride to work every day, and then I had to worry about getting home at night.

Glen told me, "Listen man, do you have to hitch a ride fourteen miles out of town to get home every night? Why don't you come stay with me at my house?"

I said, "Who are you to say that? Don't you have parents?"

He said, "Yeah, but I am the man of my house. My mom lives there, and I have no dad. I support the family."

I said, "Well, if you say so, I'll check it out."

So he snuck me into his house and it took two weeks for his mom to find out that I was living there. He just adopted me into his family, all of his brothers and sisters became my brothers and sister.

I lived there until I met Mary Alice, which was at least a couple years. After this the lady befriended me, they still all called me "brother." There are a couple of them who live in England now, and whenever they come down they look me up.

They were sad when I had to leave and go live with Mary Alice, but they still keep in touch. I see them and hang out with them and stuff like that. We're still brothers and sisters as far as I'm concerned. Even though I have my own family, they consider me part of theirs.

Marlon August

The Mugging

I lived about six years in Belize City, and I had different jobs while I was living there.

At one point, I was working with a compadre of mine who had a little juice business. He would sell juice in plastic bags. I would go to work and spend the whole day there. I'd go there and sell juice, then go for lunch, sell more juice, and go back home.

One time he asked me to come by on a weekend. I normally only worked Monday to Friday, but he was having a get together with a barbeque and drinks, a big party in his backyard.

I was there having fun, telling jokes, playing dominos. I ended up staying a little later than I thought I should have.

I had this little BMX bike. I was riding home and I got to the crossroads, and two guys showed up, one on each side of me. One of them put a gun to my head and the other one had a knife to my ribs.

They said, "Give us what you've got!"

I said, "Just take whatever, man."

My wallet was fat with papers. I always had a lot of orders from different stores. I would get all of the orders before the weekend, then on Monday I would know where I had to deliver it. When they saw the thick wallet, they must have been thinking I had a lot of money. So they grabbed my wallet and rode off.

I remembered there used to be cops that would protect the university students, so I rode my bike around and found one of those guys and I said, "Hey man, I was just mugged. These guys took my wallet at gunpoint and knifepoint."

The guy said, "Sorry to hear that, but you'll have to go file a report at the police station."

I said, "Don't you guys have a radio, or can't you go and check it out yourselves?"

He said, "We have to protect the university students."

So I went to the investigations branch and explained to the cops that I had just been robbed. The police officer looked at me and said, "Okay, sir, let me take you to look at some mugshots to see if you recognize any of them."

He took out this big book packed with photos, and sure enough one of their faces was right there. I told the cop, "That guy right there is one of them. I didn't get a good look at the other one, but this guy, I remember staring at his face with the gun right down my forehead."

The cop looked at me and said, "Okay. If you ever run into him, or see him, or hear about where he lives or anything, go ahead and give us a call."

I said, "Man, you guys are a joke, a bunch of jokes.

You're going to have me do your work? You know this guy. Why can't you just go out and look for him?"

I guess it wasn't a big enough crime. I'm not a big shot, and I didn't get cut or shot or anything. It wasn't a big enough deal for them to go out and look for him.

I lived in Belize City for a little while longer, and I was always more careful about when I would leave. I went and told my compadre, "If you want me to come and hang out from now on, you're going to have to give me a ride. I'm not going to ride my bicycle home in the dark anymore."

Run-in with a Gay Guy

When I was living in Punta Gorda. I got a job working on this bus that would leave at five in the morning from Punta Gorda and get to Belize City at about noon. The road was so bad that we would have to spend the night in this terminal in Belize City. Fortunately while I was working at the bus line my brother lived just up the road north of Belize City.

So we would meet up and spend nights over in Chetumal, Mexico. He would always say, "Hey, let's go over to Mexico and get some Mexican beer and come back tomorrow."

I said, "No problem, bro."

We would go over there and hang out with his driver. He and his driver were friends that got along very well. They would drive people there and drop them off, spend the night there, and then come back with people in the morning. I would go party with them at night. I would just have to be back by ten o'clock, and we would always get back to Belize City by then anyway.

We were hanging out one time and we went into a bar to drink some Mexican beers. It was a nice small place. We were sitting back, there were girls dancing, and we were just relaxing and enjoying our drinks.

This guy walked in with a beautiful Mexican lady and sat down at the table right next to ours and start drinking. He noticed my eyes were wandering around a bit, so he walked over to the table and asked, "Hey, would you like to dance with my lady?"

I said, "Sure, no problem."

So we started dancing, and the guy was checking me out. I thought maybe he wanted to learn the moves so he could dance with his girlfriend. Then, after the girl and I finished dancing, the guy came over and sat beside me and said, "I like you."

I said, "What?"

He said, "I like you. Why don't you come hang out with us?"

I said, "No, I'm with my brother and my friend over there."

He said, "How much would you charge me to be with you?"

I said, "What do you mean by that, you crazy son of a bitch?"

I got mad because I had never been approached by a gay guy before. I grew up in a country where it's not accepted for a guy to be gay. I drew my hand back to punch his ass out, but as soon as I had my hand back, my brother was right there to grab my elbows.

He said, "Man, don't hit a Mexican guy over here. It doesn't matter whether you're right or wrong, either way you'll go to jail."

I said, "Then let's get the hell out of here. This guy is a faggot."

He was just using that girl to bring me in. He used her to trap guys. She was just a bargirl that he hired to come out with them, then he would use her and see what he could get in return.

My brother said, "Yeah, I forgot to warn you about that. A lot of stuff like that happens here. There are cross-dressers, there are girls who look like guys, guys who look like girls. You've got to be careful."

We went to another bar because my brother didn't want me to get into trouble for hitting this guy. We just hung out and had a good time, and then we headed back him the following morning.

I had to drive back to Punta Gorda. The whole time I was just thinking about what that guy was trying to do to me, and there was this lady on the bus who was acting up.

I said to her, "Ma'am, what's the problem?"

She said, "There is not a problem. I just like seeing you. You've got a nice ass."

I said, "Thank you very much, ma'am, but I'm not interested."

That at least made me feel better after the ordeal the night before.

The Day My Brother Died

The day my brother got killed, I was living with my first ex. I had just come home from work at mid noon. My sister said, "Did you hear what happened?"

I could see that she had been crying and I said, "No…"

She started crying again and I asked, "What's wrong?"

She said, "Our brother got killed. They shot him. They found him dead on the steps up there in the cane fields."

I said, "How did this happen? We were just hanging out last night."

The night before, my brother and I had gotten a few drinks and then he had set off to do his job. He was a technician for BTL, the phone company. One of the people involved in his death was a guy who had become his employee. This guy was working for them for about six years, but he couldn't get a promotion because he didn't know what he was doing.

My brother was a sharp guy. He was skilled and knew what he was doing. Prior to working for BTL, he was a police officer for a number of years. Then he went to being a Belizean soldier for a number of years. He served until he became a Staff Sergeant. He was in training and retired after nine years of that. He was still on call to do jungle expert training and artillery training because he was a marksman and a jungle expert.

When he went to BTL to apply for a job he came highly recommended, which got him the job. This guy who they sent to be my brother's assistant, he had been working for the company for six years and he was jealous of my brother being there for only six months and becoming his boss. He was always looking for an opportunity to screw him over.

My brother used to go to this bar, and this guy had kind of introduced him to it. It was a bar in the cane fields full of hoochie mamas and stuff. My brother used to go there to hang out and drink. The owner's mistress was the one who ran the bar while the owner would stay home with his wife.

When my brother's employee heard that my brother had been hanging out there and that the girl was giving him free drinks and stuff, he got annoyed and started checking it out, asking around. Somebody told him my brother was up there.

He waited for my brother one night. The owner had given the night watchman the weekend off. He paid him off and told him to go to Honduras right away. That's where he was the night my brother was killed. My brother was shot seven times in the back, and it looked like the night watchman had done it because he was nowhere to be found since he went back to Honduras.

They kind of quit the investigation there. The cops said it was an open and shut case. BTL liked my brother so much that they had a private investigation and found out it was the owner of the place who did it. They arrested him and threw him in jail for about eight, nine months, but because of insufficient evidence they had to let him go free. He moved to the States.

My First Girlfriend

While I was working for Benny's, a couple of guys came in to buy drywall supplies.

I said to them, "What are you guys building?"

They said, "We're at the lighthouse resort."

We got into a little conversation and one of them said, "We've got two villas up. We've got a carpenter and a mason. We have everybody except a drywaller."

I said, "Well, you're talking to one."

They said, "Yeah, but you work here."

I said, "They don't own me. Make me an offer."

He said, "Okay. How much are you getting here?"

I said, "It doesn't matter. Make me an offer and I'll see if I want it."

So they made me an offer and I took it. They said, "We're leaving tomorrow on the seven o'clock flight."

They asked me to meet them at a restaurant the next day. Seeing as I had just gotten paid they day before, I jumped on the bandwagon and went off to work for them.

When I was working out there, I met my first girlfriend, Margery. I was doing the drywall for them. It was a nice day, and they put me up in a nice, air conditioned tent. The rest of the staff lived in a little shack.

All the girls there knew I was new in town, so they wanted to be with me. The one that ended up being my girlfriend was the one I saw drinking rum with these guys, just hanging out.

I said, "Hey, that's not too cool for a lady to be drinking rum. Order water or something."

But she ended up being nice to me and we hooked up.

She was a guest cook at the resort. She cooked for the staff. She used to come down after she finished cooking for the guests. She got closer to me and started bringing me guest food, pastries and stuff.

While I was working, I had no worries about the rules and regulations that applied to the rest of the staff. I hated the fact that they treated them like kids. It was the manager, his wife, and this other guy, Glen. Glen was the guy that laid down the law. The wife just stayed in the air conditioned house and never bothered anybody.

Glen would go around and check up on this house, then check up on that one. We weren't allowed to hang out, like a guy with a girl. But I broke that rule with this girl, and he heard about it. He came and yelled at her that she wasn't allowed to be hanging out with me, and to stop visiting my tent. We were all adults, just working.

One day she came down to my tent crying that the guy had been chewing her ass off about hanging out with me.

Here we were in our twenties, and he was going on like that.

I march right up to him in his office and said, "Glen, I need to talk to you."

He said, "What about?"

I said, "Let me tell you something; the next time you reprimand somebody for hanging out with somebody else, it's just going to be me and you, because I don't like that stuff. You cannot tell people who they can and can't date, or what they can and can't do in their private lives."

He said, "What in the hell is wrong with you?"

I said, "Listen, I am not working for you. I am working for your boss. You and I are on the same page. Otherwise, you're going to have a problem with me."

He said, "Well, since you're not working for me and you have a contract here, I guess I can't get you fired."

I said, "You can try, but if you get me fired I'll write you up for controlling our personal lives."

He said, "Yeah, whatever."

Anyway, things didn't go well with him and me. Within a couple weeks, the owners came down. When they came down on me, they were good for the money; they had a fridge for me with beers in it on the weekends. They didn't have any worries about when I would work or when I wouldn't work, as long as I got the job done.

Well they heard about what was going on, so they had a meeting. They talked to Glen the same way I did. They said, "Listen. You have no right over anybody's private life. You should just leave them alone. If they want to couple up, let them couple up, as long as they do their jobs."

I worked it out so that all of us happy about that. Now everybody was hanging out with each other and being friendly. I went back to work happy and finished out my contract.

The Plastic Factory

When I moved to Belize City, I got a job at a plastic packaging factory. They had a machine that could make plastic; it would turn material into whatever size plastic they wanted. They would just tell me what they needed, and I would go ahead and do it.

At first it was tough learning the machine and learning how to do the cutting, because it was designed like an airplane. It had all these different buttons for different heats and cuts and speeds and everything. It was hotter than hell in the building where I was working, because I would be sitting in there for eight to ten hours a day making plastic bags and whatnot.

Demand was high. We would have orders coming from different hotels, stores, and factories that make use of the bags in one way or another. After about two weeks of training, I was good at making plastic.

We had bakeries and stuff making orders, and sometimes they would order ten thousand bags or so. I would just sit down and not leave until I finished them. The owner became a good friend. He kept me hired there and doing that, at least until they lost their consensus due to changes in the government that took away their ability to import raw material from Mexico. They had to go back to importing readymade bags, so they needed me no more.

But before that, while I was making the bags and everything was good, I had about a year or two of experience in the business when they said, "Hey Marlon, you know what? We need to send you to Merida to learn how to repair the machine if it breaks down."

Up until then, every so often they would have to hire a guy to come in and take care of the machine if it broke down, because we had no knowledge about how to fix it.

I was working in Merida for one year. In Merida, which is Mexico, the Mexicans worked in eight hours shifts. They don't work overtime. But the factory they worked at was operational twenty-four hours a day. That meant they had three sets of workers, each group working eight hours at a time.

While I was there I was still getting paid through Belize, in Belizean salary. They just put me up there. The owner got to like me, because I would work twelve hours a day and none of his Mexican workers would do that, so he had sent a Mexican guy to fill my place in Belize while I was in Mexico.

Now the year I was there, I got really good at it. I could do anything with that machine. I could break it down into parts and then build it back up and get it going again.

I had a great time, but I couldn't stand the heat over there. I couldn't stand the lifestyle they had of eating four times a day and the food wasn't the same as what I was used to. In the neighborhood where I lived they just had a weird way of eating.

I was in downtown Merida, which is a big city. I could get whatever I wanted and it was never more than ten or fifteen miles away. I could just get on a city bus and go get some food.

Doing that several times, I would run into these gay guys. There were a whole bunch of gay guys in Merida that were after me, because I was a pretty good looking guy with curly hair. They thought, "Oh, fresh meat. We've got to try to get this guy."

I remember one night that I went into the city and I was hanging out. There was a guy from work with me; he was one of the gay guys. We partied till the wee hours of the morning and then he said, "All right, let's go back."

We got a cab, but on the way back a few of his buddies got in the cab with us and they said, "We're going to go to a party not too far from the factory and where you live."

So they took me over there, and I saw a whole bunch of guys. I said, "Hold on. I'll be right back. Let me just go take a shower and change, and then I'll be right back."

They dropped me off at the gate. The factory had tight security and electric gates, but they let me in. I told them, "Don't open the gate. Just tell those guys to get out of here, because I am not hanging out with them."

So I went to sleep.

In the morning I went to meet the owner and manager and said, "I don't want those guys to think I will play their games. I'm a straight guy. I have a girlfriend back home. I don't want to be targeted as a gay guy, so tell them to leave me alone. If you like me working here; you will do this for me."

He said, "Yes, sir."

I said, "And another thing. I want to start eating good food like rice, beans, and chicken and stuff. I can't find that around here. Even if I go to the city there isn't much of it."

He said, "Sure. I want to keep you here. I want to keep you happy. I'll take you to my house."

He had a mansion with a maid and a cook and everything. He dropped me off there for the lady to cook whatever I wanted. Every day she would make me a buffet style lunch. I'd say, "All I want is rice and chicken."

She'd say, "But I like to cook. I want to give you some nice stuff."

She would make all kinds of stuff. I'd say, "Okay, if that is what you want to do, but I am happy with just rice and chicken."

She would make the rice and chicken for me, then my boss would come and pick me up and I would go back to work.

He'd say, "Marlon, you want to play a game of pool or

something?"

He had a nice decked out pool bar in his house. We would play a game of pool every day before going back to work. He treated me like gold. Every now and then he'd take me to his jewelry store. He had a jewelry store where he sold gold and stuff.

There was a girl working there. At the time I had long curly hair, which I had in a cornrow. She loved my hair. She played with it and stuff and she said, "Can you do that with my hair?"

I said, "No. My sister did this for me before I came here."

She said, "One of these days you've got to bring your sister with you."

I stayed there for three months, working there. I went back to Belize for a week, then got back to work. Whenever I would leave she would get sad and she would always say, "One of these days I will come visit you down in Belize and have your sister do my hair."

I said, "Sure. We'd be glad to have you, and she'd be glad to do that for you."

But that never happened.

A little bit after that I went back to work in the factory in Belize. Shortly after I got back was when the owners lost their ability to import raw materials.

They said, "Marlon, we're so sorry that we're going to have to lay you off. The factory won't be operating because we can't import raw material. We have to import readymade bags. Since my cousin is the one who delivers, I can't give you that job, but we can try to find something for you." Her husband at the time was a general manager at Shell Belize, which is a gas depot in Belize. She said, "We can try to fit you in there."

I said, "No, that's all right. Thank you for having me work for you, and thank you for the way you treated me."

They would bring me drinks and bread and invite my

family and me over for drinks and food. I appreciated all they did for me, but at the same time I didn't need them to pity me. I said, "You did what you had to do. The government screwed you guys over. It's not your fault. I can find another job."

I managed to get a job at a foam factory as a chemist, mixing chemicals to make foam and then dumping it out into a plywood box, and then we would cut it to size whatever the specifications of the order were.

I worked there for about two years, then I started getting sick. I got bronchitis because of the smoke that the chemicals let off. The Lebanese owner wouldn't provide us with proper gas masks and equipment for working. A few other guys got sick too. I got bronchitis, one guy had full blown tuberculosis, the other guy had asthma.

I went to the health department to complain about how they were treating us there, and how they were destroying out lungs. The health guy came over and the boss pulled him into his office, paid him off, and had him point at the one who reported him.

He called me up to the office a little bit after that, with his gun sitting on the table, to tell me that I shouldn't have done that because he was a high man in society. It was true. He was a Lebanese ambassador to Belize.

I said, "Yes, sir. I know that, but I'm not going to let you humiliate me. If that is the way you're going to treat me then I am quitting today, because you're not going to take your gun and scare me off. You are wrong to do what you do."

After that I went to Placentia. My girlfriend at the time was living and working down there, so I went to join her. I got a job there working at a resort as a bartender. The girl who was the manager there was from my hometown. She was quite happy to have me.

We used to throw parties on the weekends. We'd have live bands and DJs. I would take care of that myself. I would collect fees at the door, then I would go to my bar and start bartending while the party was going on and people were having a good time. The boss lady would go home and I would stay there half the night, until maybe two or three in the morning.

She had me living in a three bedroom house that she provided. Most of the guys here were from Belize City. To make it more affordable for them, I would let them stay in my house. I would sleep on the couch, and they could use the three bedrooms.

At the end of the parties I would sometimes have three or four thousand dollars on me. I would stuff it in my pants and then sleep on my stomach to keep it safe. I wouldn't trust the guys I was with to put it anywhere else. In the morning I would take it to my boss. Her name was Ruth.

I said, "Ruth, this is what we made last night."

She would say, "Thank you, Marlon. Take this. You did good."

Placentia is a little village that didn't have any banks or anything, so she had to do all of her banking in Dangriga, which was nearby. It's just a flght from Placentia to Dangriga, or a long drive. She used to send me on a flight to Dangriga whenever she needed to deposit money.

There was this girl working with her there. They went to high school together. She got jealous of the relationship Ruth and I had.

She would say, "You're going to trust that guy? Ruth, why don't you trust me? I've been your friend all these years and went to school with you and everything."

Ruth would say, "Yeah, but Karen, Marlon is pushing my business. That's the reason I trust him. If you think he'll steal from me, you're wrong. And if he does, it will only be one time."

I would never have stolen, because I had a good gig going on. She would pay my fair, and I would get to stay at a fancy hotel and resort. I got to have lunch between my flights back and forth. Then I would come back and start working again.

Before that, these girls would just sit in the bar and gossip. People would be walking down the sidewalk, and these girls would just pray that they would go into their bar rather than try to bring them in. I would always try to grab them by saying, "Hey, you can grab a bite to eat right here." They would sometimes get mad at me for bringing in business, which made it so they couldn't sit and gossip.

After about a year of that they started hating me for pushing business and making them work. Eventually I said to Ruth, "You know what, I'm going to move away from here. I'm going to go back to Belize City and try my luck there again."

When I moved back to Belize City she said, "If things pick up again, I'll call you. If you need it."

As soon as I got back to Belize City I got a job as a drywall salesman at Benny's Home Depot, which is the biggest in Belize. It's like the Home Depot of the States.

Marlon B. August was born in the wild western town of San Ignacio, Belize to Claribell Burns and Zachariahs August. He grew up in the rainforest in the village of Espenanza. His dad was a farmer of both livestock and agriculture so Marlon worked hard from a very young age. He left home to go to work at the age of thirteen and began his life of adventure. Marlon has retained his mother's upbringing and the way she lived as a herbiest (herbalist) and has helped many people with his extensive native herbal knowledge. He has lived in every corner of Belize and frequently takes new friends on tours of Belize's Mayan ruins, cave tubing and along the Medicine Trail in the rainforest where he grew up.

18228927R00076